The Cloud Revolution:
Powering the Digital Age

By

Dexter L. Crawford

TABLE OF CONTENTS

CHAPTER I
Introduction

A. The Evolving Landscape of Technology and Data

In the ever-changing world of technology, we find ourselves at the precipice of a monumental transformation: the cloud revolution. Over the past few decades, our dependence on digital technologies has skyrocketed, permeating almost every aspect of our lives. From the way we communicate and conduct business to how we access information and entertain ourselves, technology has become an inseparable part of modern existence.

This pervasive integration of technology has been fueled by the explosion of data. With each passing day, an inconceivable amount of data is generated, from social media interactions and online transactions to the vast network of interconnected devices forming the Internet of Things (IoT). This data boom presents both incredible opportunities and daunting challenges for individuals, businesses, and societies at large.

Amid this data deluge, cloud computing emerged as a transformative force, reshaping the way we store, process, and utilize information. The cloud has not only revolutionized the IT industry but has also unleashed unprecedented potential for innovation across all sectors. By leveraging the cloud's vast resources and flexibility, companies can now embark on ambitious projects, scale rapidly, and access cutting-edge technologies without major upfront investments.

The cloud revolution is not merely a technical paradigm shift; it signifies a fundamental change in how we approach and perceive technology. It heralds an era where barriers to entry are lowered, where startups can disrupt established industries, and where collaboration and sharing become the norm. As traditional data centers fade into the background, the cloud emerges as the backbone of the digital age, driving progress at an unprecedented pace.

In this book, we will delve deep into the essence of the cloud revolution, exploring its historical roots, its impact on businesses and societies, and the challenges it brings forth. We will uncover the underlying principles of cloud computing, demystify its different service models and deployment options, and examine real-world success stories that showcase the immense power of the cloud.

Moreover, we cannot ignore the ethical and security considerations entwined with the cloud's omnipresence. As we embrace the cloud's capabilities, we must address concerns about data privacy, transparency, and responsible data usage. The cloud revolution calls for a balance between convenience and protecting sensitive information, ensuring that our digital progress respects the boundaries of ethics and human rights.

The journey into the cloud revolution is not one of mere technological prowess but also of profound implications for our society's future. As we peer into the horizon, we catch glimpses of edge computing, quantum computing, and sustainable cloud initiatives. These emerging trends beckon us to explore new possibilities, challenging us to remain vigilant about potential pitfalls while striving for a digital world that uplifts us all.

In the chapters that follow, we invite you to embark on this enlightening expedition, where we will navigate the complexities of the cloud revolution, discover its manifold implications, and chart a course towards a more connected, innovative, and inclusive digital age. As the clouds gather on the technological horizon, it is time to harness their power and embark on a journey of transformative change.

B. The Rise of Cloud Computing

In the annals of technological advancement, few innovations have been as revolutionary and transformative as cloud computing. As we step into the digital age, the rise of cloud computing stands tall as a defining moment that reshaped the way we interact with technology, store data, and conduct business. This chapter delves into the genesis and ascendancy of cloud computing, shedding light on the forces that propelled it to the forefront of the digital revolution.

The roots of cloud computing can be traced back to the early seeds of the internet. In the 1960s, visionary thinkers conceptualized the idea of a "galactic computer network," envisioning a future where interconnected computers would enable information-sharing on a global scale. This prescient notion laid the foundation for the interconnected digital world we inhabit today.

The true catalyst for the rise of cloud computing, however, can be attributed to the convergence of several key factors in the late 20th and early 21st centuries. First and foremost was the exponential growth of data. As businesses and individuals generated an unprecedented amount of information, the need for scalable and cost-effective storage solutions became apparent.

Around the same time, advancements in virtualization and data center technologies were gaining momentum. These breakthroughs allowed for the efficient partitioning of physical hardware, enabling multiple virtual machines to run on a single server. This marked a paradigm shift in computing, as it vastly improved resource utilization and operational flexibility.

Then came the crucial moment: the launch of Amazon Web Services (AWS) in 2006. AWS introduced the concept of Infrastructure as a Service (IaaS), offering businesses the ability to rent computing resources over the internet. This move not only democratized access to computing power but also established the modern cloud computing model, where resources could be provisioned on-demand, scaling up or down as needed.

As the success of AWS became evident, other tech giants swiftly followed suit. Microsoft Azure, Google Cloud Platform (GCP), and other major players entered the cloud arena, each offering their unique suite of cloud services. The competition intensified, spurring rapid innovation and driving down prices, making cloud computing even more accessible to businesses of all sizes.

The rise of cloud computing also revolutionized software development and deployment. The emergence of Platform as a Service (PaaS) and Software as a Service (SaaS) models allowed developers to focus on creating applications without worrying about the underlying infrastructure. This newfound agility accelerated the pace of software development, leading to a plethora of innovative applications that catered to diverse user needs.

Today, the cloud is the backbone of the digital economy, empowering businesses to thrive in an era of digital disruption. From startups to multinational corporations, organizations leverage the cloud's potential to stay competitive, achieve global reach, and pioneer new frontiers. The cloud's elasticity, reliability, and ease of scalability have become indispensable assets in navigating an ever-evolving technological landscape.

As we embark on this journey through the cloud revolution, we will explore its multifaceted impact on industries, societies, and individuals. The cloud's rise marks not only a turning point in the history of computing but also a testament to human ingenuity and the relentless pursuit of progress. Let us now dive into the depths of the cloud's transformative power and unravel the mysteries that lie ahead in the digital age.

C. The Promise of the Cloud Revolution

In an age where technology has become the beating heart of our daily lives, the cloud revolution emerges as a beacon of promise, illuminating the path to a more connected, efficient, and innovative world. The ever-expanding landscape of digital possibilities presents us with unprecedented opportunities, and the cloud stands at the forefront, ready to unlock the full potential of this brave new era.

At its core, the promise of the cloud revolution lies in its ability to transcend barriers. Gone are the days when organizations were restricted by the limitations of their on-premises infrastructure. With the cloud, businesses can now break free from the shackles of physical hardware, liberating themselves to explore new horizons and expand their reach beyond borders.

The cloud promises unparalleled scalability, allowing businesses to scale their operations seamlessly to meet surging demands or adjust to varying market conditions. No longer constrained by static server capacities, enterprises can dynamically allocate resources as needed, optimizing performance and cost-efficiency in real-time. This newfound agility empowers companies to be more responsive, adaptive, and resilient in the face of dynamic market forces.

Moreover, the cloud revolution heralds a new era of collaboration and innovation. With data and services residing in a shared, virtual realm, collaboration between teams and organizations becomes frictionless. Geographical boundaries fade away, fostering global partnerships and harnessing diverse talents for collective progress. Startups and entrepreneurs are now empowered to focus on their core competencies without worrying about building complex infrastructure, enabling them to unleash their creativity and pursue ambitious visions with limited upfront investment.

For consumers, the promise of the cloud revolution translates into a seamless and interconnected digital experience. From streaming media and social networking to e-commerce and smart home devices, the cloud plays a pivotal role in delivering personalized, on-demand services that enrich our daily lives. The cloud's omnipresence ensures that information is always at our fingertips, accessible from any device, anytime, and anywhere.

The cloud revolution has also ushered in an era of democratization. Technology that was once accessible only to large corporations with substantial budgets is now available to startups, small businesses, and individuals alike. Cloud services come in various forms, from Infrastructure as a Service (IaaS) and Platform as a Service (PaaS) to Software as a Service (SaaS), catering to diverse needs and budgets. This democratization of technology fosters a level playing field, allowing innovative ideas to thrive regardless of an entity's size or financial muscle.

In addition to the promises of convenience and efficiency, the cloud revolution opens doors to cutting-edge technologies such as artificial intelligence, machine learning, and big data analytics. By leveraging cloud-based resources, businesses can harness the immense power of these technologies to gain deeper insights, optimize operations, and make data-driven decisions that drive meaningful outcomes.

As we embark on this exploration of the cloud revolution, we will delve into its inner workings, the challenges it confronts, and the ethical considerations that accompany its immense potential. Together, we will traverse the landscapes of cloud-native technologies, the burgeoning IoT ecosystem, and the ever-expanding frontiers of digital innovation.

The promise of the cloud revolution is not a distant vision; it is a reality unfolding before our eyes. With the power of the cloud at our disposal, we are poised to embrace a future where imagination knows no bounds and where the digital age serves as a gateway to a better, more connected, and inclusive world. Join us as we embark on this transformative journey, where the cloud revolution empowers us to shape a future that knows no limits.

CHAPTER II
The Foundation of Cloud Computing

A. Understanding Cloud Computing Principles

In the digital landscape of today, cloud computing has emerged as a game-changing paradigm that revolutionizes how we store, access, and process data. At its essence, cloud computing is the provision of on-demand computing resources over the internet, granting users the flexibility to scale their operations without the burden of managing physical infrastructure. This chapter unveils the core principles that underpin cloud computing, as well as the key characteristics that differentiate it from traditional IT models.

Definition and Key Characteristics

Cloud computing is a revolutionary approach to computing that enables users to access a pool of shared computing resources, including processing power, storage, and networking, delivered as a service over the internet. The hallmark feature of cloud computing is its elasticity, allowing resources to be rapidly provisioned or de-provisioned based on changing demands. Users pay only for the resources they consume, making it a cost-effective alternative to traditional, on-premises infrastructure.

One of the key characteristics of cloud computing is its on-demand self-service nature. Users can easily provision resources and manage their usage through a web-based interface or API, giving them unprecedented control and autonomy over their computing needs. This accessibility empowers businesses to respond quickly to market demands and capitalize on opportunities as they arise.

Cloud computing also boasts broad network access, enabling users to access services and applications over the internet from a variety of devices, such as laptops, smartphones, and tablets. This flexibility fosters a seamless user experience, allowing individuals to work and collaborate from any location with an internet connection.

Additionally, cloud computing exhibits resource pooling, a fundamental concept wherein multiple users share the same physical resources. Virtualization technologies play a vital role in achieving resource pooling, as they allow multiple virtual machines (VMs) or containers to run on a single physical server, maximizing resource utilization and efficiency.

Another key aspect of cloud computing is rapid elasticity, which enables resources to scale up or down dynamically in response to workload fluctuations. This elasticity ensures that applications and services can handle varying levels of traffic without compromising performance or incurring unnecessary costs during periods of low demand.

Types of Cloud Services (SaaS, PaaS, IaaS)

Cloud computing services are typically categorized into three main models: Software as a Service (SaaS), Platform as a Service (PaaS), and Infrastructure as a Service (IaaS). Each model caters to different levels of control and responsibility for users.

- Software as a Service (SaaS): SaaS delivers software applications over the internet on a subscription basis. Users can access these applications directly through a web browser, eliminating the need for local installations or complex configurations. Popular examples of SaaS include web-based email services, cloud-based office suites, and customer relationship management (CRM) systems.

- Platform as a Service (PaaS): PaaS provides a platform that allows developers to build, deploy, and manage applications without the complexities of underlying infrastructure management. Developers can focus solely on coding and application logic, while the PaaS provider takes care of the underlying hardware and software infrastructure. PaaS accelerates the development process, reduces time-to-market, and promotes collaboration among development teams.

- Infrastructure as a Service (IaaS): IaaS offers virtualized computing resources over the internet. Users have control over these resources and can deploy and manage virtual machines, storage, and networking according to their specific needs. IaaS provides the flexibility to scale resources up or down as required, making it an ideal choice for businesses with variable workloads or those seeking to migrate existing on-premises infrastructure to the cloud.

Cloud Deployment Models (Public, Private, Hybrid)

Cloud deployment models define how cloud services are hosted, managed, and accessed. The three primary deployment models are public, private, and hybrid clouds, each tailored to specific organizational requirements.

- Public Cloud: Public clouds are services provided by third-party cloud service providers, offering resources to multiple organizations and individuals over the internet. These clouds are hosted and managed by the service provider, and users benefit from economies of scale, cost-effectiveness, and the ease of accessing services on a pay-as-you-go basis. Public clouds are ideal for businesses and individuals seeking an agile and cost-efficient solution without the need for significant upfront investments.

- Private Cloud: Private clouds are dedicated infrastructures exclusively utilized by a single organization. They can be hosted on-premises or by a third-party provider, depending on the organization's preferences and security requirements. Private clouds offer greater control, customization, and security, making them suitable for organizations with strict compliance or data governance regulations, such as government agencies and enterprises handling sensitive data.

- Hybrid Cloud: Hybrid clouds combine elements of both public and private clouds, creating a cohesive and integrated computing environment. Organizations can take advantage of the scalability and cost-efficiency of public clouds while keeping sensitive data or critical workloads in a private cloud for enhanced security and control. Hybrid clouds offer the flexibility to move workloads between public and private environments as needed, optimizing resource allocation and application performance.

In conclusion, understanding the principles of cloud computing is pivotal in grasping the transformative power of this revolutionary technology. The concepts of on-demand self-service, resource pooling, and rapid elasticity have unlocked unprecedented opportunities for businesses and individuals to innovate, collaborate, and thrive in the dynamic digital age. Moreover, the diverse cloud service models and deployment options empower users to tailor their cloud strategies according to their unique needs and objectives, ensuring that the cloud revolution is a customizable journey towards a more connected and agile future.

B. Historical Evolution of Cloud Computing

Early Concepts and Origins

The roots of cloud computing can be traced back to the visionary ideas of computer scientist John McCarthy in the 1960s. He envisioned a "utility computing" model where computing resources would be accessible akin to electricity grids. Despite the futuristic vision, the technology of the time could not support such a concept, and it remained an idea ahead of its time.

The term "cloud computing" itself was coined much later in the 1990s by Ramnath Chellappa, who used it to describe a new paradigm of delivering computing resources as a service over the internet. The cloud metaphor referred to the abstraction of complex infrastructure, hiding it from users and representing it as a cloud in network diagrams.

Milestones and Breakthroughs

The evolution of cloud computing gained momentum in the early 2000s, propelled by significant breakthroughs and innovations:

a. Virtualization: The advent of virtualization technology in the late 1990s and early 2000s played a pivotal role in shaping cloud computing. Technologies like VMware allowed for the creation of virtual machines, enabling multiple operating systems and applications to run on a single physical server. This efficient resource utilization set the stage for the scalability of cloud services.

b. Amazon Web Services (AWS): In 2006, AWS, launched by Amazon.com, marked a turning point in cloud computing history. AWS introduced the concept of Infrastructure as a Service (IaaS), offering computing resources on a pay-as-you-go basis. It provided a scalable and cost-effective solution for businesses to access on-demand computing power without the need for significant upfront investments.

c. Platform as a Service (PaaS) and Software as a Service (SaaS): Following the success of IaaS, cloud providers expanded their offerings to include PaaS and SaaS models. PaaS allowed developers to build, deploy, and manage applications without worrying about underlying infrastructure, while SaaS delivered software applications directly over the internet. This ushered in an era of application-centric cloud services.

d. Google and Microsoft's Entry: Google launched Google App Engine in 2008, providing a platform for building and hosting web applications. Around the same time, Microsoft unveiled its cloud offering, Windows Azure, which later evolved into Microsoft Azure. These entries from tech giants solidified the cloud computing market and ignited fierce competition among cloud service providers.

e. OpenStack: OpenStack, an open-source cloud computing platform, emerged in 2010, backed by a consortium of technology companies. It aimed to provide an alternative to proprietary cloud solutions and foster interoperability among various cloud providers. OpenStack's community-driven approach contributed significantly to the growth of cloud adoption.

Adoption by Businesses and Industries

As cloud computing matured and demonstrated its capabilities, businesses across various industries started recognizing its potential benefits. Cloud computing provided organizations with the agility to scale their operations quickly, reduce IT costs, and focus on their core competencies.

Small and medium-sized enterprises (SMEs) were among the first to adopt cloud services due to the low barrier to entry and cost-effectiveness. Startups found the cloud particularly advantageous, as it allowed them to launch and test new business ideas rapidly without substantial capital investment in infrastructure.

Large enterprises soon followed suit, leveraging the cloud to optimize their IT infrastructure, streamline business processes, and drive innovation. The scalability and flexibility of the cloud made it possible for companies to handle massive volumes of data and meet surges in demand during peak times, all while avoiding the need for significant upfront investments in hardware.

Industries with variable workloads, such as e-commerce, media, and online services, found the cloud particularly appealing. Cloud computing allowed them to cater to fluctuating customer demands efficiently, ensuring a seamless user experience and enhancing customer satisfaction.

The cloud also played a crucial role in research and development, providing researchers and scientists with the computational power required for complex simulations, data analysis, and cutting-edge experiments. Moreover, the cloud facilitated collaboration among geographically dispersed teams, accelerating the pace of scientific discoveries and breakthroughs.

Healthcare, finance, and government sectors, which deal with sensitive and confidential data, initially approached cloud adoption with caution due to security and compliance concerns. However, as cloud providers improved their security protocols and obtained certifications to meet industry-specific regulations, these sectors also started to embrace cloud computing as a means to modernize their operations and improve service delivery.

In conclusion, the historical evolution of cloud computing has been a journey marked by visionary ideas, transformative breakthroughs, and widespread adoption. From its early conceptualization as a utility computing model to becoming a fundamental pillar of the digital age, cloud computing has redefined how businesses operate, collaborate, and innovate. The milestones achieved by pioneers like AWS, Google, and Microsoft have paved the way for a competitive and dynamic cloud computing market that continues to evolve, driving digital transformation across industries and pushing the boundaries of what is possible in the connected world.

CHAPTER III
Empowering Digital Transformation

A. The Impact of Cloud on Businesses

The advent of cloud computing has ignited a paradigm shift in the way businesses operate, unleashing a wave of digital transformation that transcends industries and revolutionizes workflows. This chapter explores the profound impact of the cloud on businesses and how it has become a catalyst for innovation, agility, and competitive advantage.

Enhancing Agility and Scalability

One of the most significant benefits that the cloud brings to businesses is its inherent agility and scalability. In traditional IT setups, businesses faced challenges when it came to rapidly adapting to changing demands or accommodating sudden surges in user traffic. Scaling on-premises infrastructure could be time-consuming and costly, often leading to operational bottlenecks.

With cloud computing, agility becomes a competitive advantage. Businesses can provision additional computing resources in a matter of minutes or scale down during quieter periods, optimizing costs and performance. Cloud service providers offer a vast pool of resources that can be dynamically allocated based on real-time requirements. As a result, businesses can respond promptly to market trends, seasonal variations, or unexpected spikes in user demand without the need for significant capital investments.

Moreover, cloud services empower businesses to expand their global reach seamlessly. The cloud's network of data centers located across the world enables companies to deliver content and services to users in various geographic regions, reducing latency and enhancing user experience. This geographic diversity allows organizations to reach new markets swiftly and tap into untapped opportunities beyond their physical borders.

Driving Innovation and Competitive Advantage

In the digital age, the ability to innovate rapidly is a key driver of competitive advantage. Cloud computing has become an enabler of innovation, as it provides businesses with the technological foundation to explore and experiment with new ideas without being hampered by infrastructure constraints.

Through Platform as a Service (PaaS) offerings, developers gain access to a plethora of tools, frameworks, and development environments. This democratization of technology empowers developers to focus on building applications and services, leveraging pre-built components and APIs to expedite development cycles. As a result, businesses can bring new features, products, and services to market faster, beating competitors and staying ahead of the curve.

Cloud-based collaboration tools further foster innovation by facilitating real-time collaboration among distributed teams. Remote teams can collaborate seamlessly, sharing ideas, data, and knowledge, driving a collective effort towards achieving common goals. This collaborative approach breaks down barriers and silos, allowing for a more dynamic and creative problem-solving process.

Additionally, the cloud enables the integration of cutting-edge technologies, such as artificial intelligence

(AI), machine learning (ML), and Internet of Things (IoT), into business operations. These technologies can yield valuable insights, enhance decision-making processes, and streamline operations, all of which contribute to an organization's competitive advantage in a rapidly evolving market.

Accelerating Time-to-Market for Products and Services

In the fast-paced digital economy, time-to-market is a critical success factor for businesses. Cloud computing significantly accelerates the time-to-market for products and services, enabling businesses to capitalize on market opportunities swiftly.

With the cloud's Infrastructure as a Service (IaaS) and PaaS models, businesses can quickly set up development and testing environments. This rapid provisioning of resources expedites the software development lifecycle, reducing development cycles from months to weeks or even days.

Moreover, cloud-based continuous integration and continuous deployment (CI/CD) pipelines facilitate an automated and streamlined process for deploying software updates and new features. Developers can push code changes to production rapidly and reliably, eliminating manual intervention and reducing the risk of errors.

Cloud-based Software as a Service (SaaS) solutions further accelerate the deployment of enterprise applications. Businesses can adopt ready-to-use cloud-based applications, eliminating the need for extensive installation and configuration processes. This swift adoption of SaaS applications empowers employees to be productive immediately, reducing downtime and increasing overall efficiency.

In conclusion, the impact of cloud computing on businesses is multi-faceted, transforming the way organizations operate and thrive in the digital age. The cloud's agility and scalability empower businesses to respond nimbly to changing market dynamics, while the ability to drive innovation and embrace cutting-edge technologies fuels their competitive advantage. Perhaps most crucially, cloud computing accelerates time-to-market, enabling businesses to capitalize on opportunities swiftly and shape their digital destinies with unparalleled speed and efficiency. As the cloud revolution unfolds, businesses stand at the precipice of a new era of growth and success, where the cloud becomes the backbone of their digital transformation journey.

B. Cloud's Role in the Digital Ecosystem

As businesses and industries journey through the digital transformation era, the cloud emerges as a linchpin in the digital ecosystem, empowering organizations to harness the full potential of emerging technologies and driving innovation at an unprecedented scale. This chapter explores the pivotal role of the cloud in facilitating the integration and utilization of transformative technologies, such as big data and analytics, Internet of Things (IoT), and artificial intelligence (AI) and machine learning (ML).

Big Data and Analytics in the Cloud

The advent of big data has revolutionized how organizations capture, store, and analyze vast volumes of information generated every second. Big data analytics plays a pivotal role in transforming raw data into actionable insights, empowering businesses to make informed decisions and gain a competitive edge.

The cloud provides the ideal infrastructure for big data and analytics processes. Its massive storage capabilities and elastic computing resources enable businesses to ingest, store, and process enormous amounts of data cost-effectively and efficiently. Cloud-based data lakes and data warehouses serve as centralized repositories for various data types, allowing businesses to consolidate disparate data sources for comprehensive analysis.

Cloud-based analytics tools and platforms further empower organizations to perform complex data processing and analysis without the need for significant upfront investments in hardware and software. Cloud-native analytics solutions offer a wide array of pre-built algorithms, AI-powered data discovery tools, and data visualization capabilities, democratizing data insights and making them accessible to users across the organization.

The cloud's scalability also proves invaluable in handling fluctuating data volumes, enabling businesses to accommodate sudden spikes in data influx during seasonal promotions, marketing campaigns, or events. This dynamic scaling ensures that big data analytics processes remain responsive and performant even during periods of high demand.

IoT and the Cloud's Interconnectedness

The Internet of Things (IoT) has ushered in a new era of connectivity, where a vast network of interconnected devices collects and shares data in real-time. IoT applications span across industries, including smart cities, industrial automation, healthcare monitoring, and smart homes.

The cloud plays a central role in the IoT ecosystem by providing a robust and scalable platform for managing and processing IoT data. IoT devices collect massive amounts of data continuously, necessitating cloud-based solutions that can accommodate this constant influx of information. Cloud-based IoT platforms offer the ability to ingest, process, and analyze IoT data streams, empowering businesses to derive meaningful insights and take immediate actions.

Furthermore, the cloud's global network of data centers ensures low-latency data transmission and response times, critical for real-time IoT applications. By leveraging the cloud's distributed infrastructure, organizations can ensure that IoT data is processed in proximity to the devices, minimizing delays and optimizing performance.

Security is a paramount concern in the IoT landscape, and the cloud addresses these concerns through robust authentication, encryption, and access control mechanisms. Cloud providers invest heavily in security measures, offering businesses peace of mind when it comes to safeguarding their IoT data and devices from potential threats.

Artificial Intelligence and Machine Learning in the Cloud

Artificial Intelligence (AI) and Machine Learning (ML) are transforming industries by enabling advanced automation, predictive analytics, and personalized user experiences. AI-driven applications are becoming ubiquitous, from virtual assistants and chatbots to recommendation engines and autonomous vehicles.

The cloud has become the bedrock for AI and ML development and deployment. Cloud providers offer a rich ecosystem of AI/ML services and tools, allowing businesses to build and deploy AI models without the need for specialized hardware or expertise. This democratization of AI empowers businesses of all sizes to incorporate AI-driven features into their products and services.

Cloud-based AI services encompass Natural Language Processing (NLP), computer vision, speech recognition, and more. These services are readily accessible through APIs, enabling developers to integrate AI capabilities into their applications with minimal effort.

Additionally, the cloud's computing power and scalability are paramount for training AI models, which often require vast computational resources. The cloud's elastic infrastructure allows organizations to scale up or down based on their AI workloads, optimizing costs and time-to-value.

AI and ML models also benefit from continuous learning, a process known as model training and retraining. The cloud's flexibility enables organizations to implement iterative model training workflows, ensuring that AI systems continuously improve and remain up-to-date with changing data patterns and user behavior.

In conclusion, the cloud's role in the digital ecosystem is pivotal, acting as a catalyst for businesses to unlock the potential of transformative technologies such as big data analytics, IoT, and AI/ML. By providing elastic and scalable infrastructure, the cloud empowers organizations to handle vast volumes of data, seamlessly connect IoT devices, and leverage AI/ML capabilities for informed decision-making and personalized experiences.

CHAPTER IV
Challenges and Security in the Cloud Era

A. Addressing Concerns about Data Privacy

In the rapidly evolving landscape of the cloud era, concerns about data privacy have become a focal point for businesses and individuals alike. As data becomes the lifeblood of the digital age, protecting sensitive information and ensuring compliance with regulations have become paramount. This chapter delves into the challenges posed by data privacy in the cloud and explores best practices for addressing these concerns.

Compliance and Regulations

Data privacy regulations and compliance requirements vary across countries and industries, posing a complex challenge for businesses operating in a global digital economy. One of the most well-known and far-reaching regulations is the European Union's General Data Protection Regulation (GDPR), which aims to protect the personal data of EU citizens and residents.

GDPR compliance requires businesses to implement robust data protection measures, ensure explicit consent for data processing, and promptly report data breaches to the relevant authorities. Failure to comply with GDPR can lead to substantial fines, tarnishing an organization's reputation and impacting its bottom line.

Apart from GDPR, numerous other data privacy regulations exist worldwide, such as the California Consumer Privacy Act (CCPA) in the United States and the Personal Information Protection Act (PIPA) in Japan. Adhering to these diverse regulations requires a comprehensive understanding of regional laws and meticulous planning to create a harmonized data privacy strategy.

Cloud service providers play a critical role in ensuring compliance by offering a range of security features and certifications. Businesses must carefully assess the security and privacy controls of their chosen cloud providers to verify compliance with relevant regulations and industry standards.

Data Breaches and Security Incidents

The rise of cloud computing has also introduced new security challenges, including the risk of data breaches and security incidents. Despite the robust security measures implemented by cloud providers, no system is entirely immune to cyber threats.

Data breaches can occur due to various factors, such as weak passwords, misconfigurations, or sophisticated cyberattacks. When a data breach occurs, sensitive information may be exposed, leading to severe consequences for individuals and organizations.

Cloud customers share the responsibility for securing their data. Implementing security best practices, such as robust access controls, encryption, and multi-factor authentication, is vital to protect sensitive data from unauthorized access. Regular security audits and vulnerability assessments are essential for identifying and addressing potential weaknesses in cloud infrastructure.

Businesses must also have incident response plans in place to handle security breaches effectively. A well-defined incident response plan helps minimize the impact of a breach, facilitates rapid containment, and supports recovery efforts. Cloud providers often offer incident response support as part of their services, collaborating with businesses to mitigate the effects of security incidents.

Best Practices for Data Protection

To address data privacy concerns effectively, businesses should adopt a proactive approach to data protection. Here are some best practices to safeguard data in the cloud era:

a. Data Classification: Classify data based on sensitivity levels to ensure appropriate security controls are applied. Not all data requires the same level of protection, and a data classification framework aids in prioritizing security efforts.

b. Encryption: Implement encryption for data both at rest and in transit. Encryption safeguards data from unauthorized access, even if a security breach occurs.

c. Access Controls: Enforce strong access controls and authentication mechanisms to limit data access to authorized personnel only. Use role-based access controls (RBAC) to ensure users have the necessary permissions based on their roles.

d. Regular Backups: Perform regular backups of critical data to ensure data availability and recoverability in case of data loss or corruption.

e. Employee Training: Educate employees about data privacy best practices and cybersecurity awareness. Human error remains a significant factor in data breaches, and a well-informed workforce can serve as a strong defense against potential threats.

f. Data Retention Policies: Establish data retention policies to determine the period for which data should be stored. Regularly review and dispose of data that is no longer required, reducing the attack surface for potential breaches.

g. Third-Party Assessments: Conduct regular assessments of cloud service providers to ensure they adhere to security standards and comply with data protection regulations.

In conclusion, addressing concerns about data privacy is of paramount importance in the cloud era. Businesses must navigate a complex landscape of data privacy regulations, proactively safeguard their data, and be prepared to respond swiftly to security incidents. By embracing best practices for data protection, organizations can build trust with customers, foster a culture of privacy, and leverage the cloud's transformative potential with confidence. A comprehensive and strategic approach to data privacy ensures that the cloud remains a secure and empowering platform for digital transformation in the interconnected world of tomorrow.

B. Cloud Governance and Risk Management

As businesses increasingly rely on the cloud to power their digital transformation journeys, effective cloud governance and risk management have emerged as critical factors for success. This chapter explores the challenges organizations face in managing cloud resources, selecting and managing cloud vendors, and ensuring disaster recovery and business continuity in the cloud environment.

Ensuring Cloud Cost-Effectiveness

While the cloud offers tremendous benefits, it also introduces cost-related challenges. Without proper governance, cloud costs can escalate rapidly, leading to unexpected expenditures and budget overruns. To ensure cloud cost-effectiveness, businesses must adopt a disciplined approach to cloud resource management.

Cloud cost optimization begins with a comprehensive understanding of cloud pricing models. Cloud providers typically offer pay-as-you-go pricing, which provides flexibility but requires careful monitoring of resource usage. By leveraging tools provided by cloud vendors and third-party cost management platforms, organizations can track resource consumption, identify cost anomalies, and optimize spending.

Rightsizing cloud resources is another crucial aspect of cost management. Evaluating workload performance and resource requirements enables businesses to allocate resources efficiently, eliminating underutilized or oversized instances. Adopting reserved instances or spot instances, where applicable, can lead to significant cost savings without compromising performance.

Cloud cost governance also involves setting up budget limits and alerts to prevent unexpected expenses. By defining spending thresholds and receiving real-time notifications, organizations can take proactive measures to control cloud costs before they spiral out of control.

Vendor Selection and Management

Selecting the right cloud vendor is a critical decision that profoundly impacts an organization's cloud journey. With numerous cloud service providers in the market, each offering a diverse set of services, businesses must carefully evaluate their options based on their unique requirements and long-term goals.

Vendor selection begins with a thorough assessment of the vendor's reliability, performance, security, and compliance track record. Evaluating a vendor's service level agreements (SLAs) is crucial to understanding the level of service and uptime commitment. Additionally, businesses must consider the geographical locations of data centers, data residency requirements, and the vendor's ability to meet regulatory compliance obligations.

Managing cloud vendors effectively requires proactive communication and collaboration. Establishing strong relationships with vendors fosters transparency and facilitates joint efforts in addressing challenges and optimizing services. Regular performance reviews and governance meetings help ensure that vendors deliver on their promises and align their services with evolving business needs.

Vendor lock-in is a potential concern in the cloud environment. Businesses should carefully assess the portability of their data and applications in case they decide to switch cloud providers. Adopting cloud-agnostic architectures and leveraging open standards can mitigate the risk of vendor lock-in and provide the flexibility to switch between cloud providers as needed.

Disaster Recovery and Business Continuity in the Cloud

Disaster recovery and business continuity are integral components of cloud governance and risk management. The cloud's resilience and redundancy capabilities can be leveraged to build robust disaster recovery (DR) strategies that ensure data and applications remain available even during adverse events.

Cloud-based disaster recovery leverages geo-distributed data centers to replicate data and applications across multiple regions. This geographical diversity minimizes the impact of regional outages, ensuring high availability of critical services to users.

Automated backup and snapshot policies enhance data protection and facilitate rapid recovery. Cloud providers offer native backup and recovery services that simplify the process of creating and managing backups. Automated snapshots allow businesses to capture point-in-time copies of their data, enabling quick restoration of systems to a known state.

The cloud also supports continuous data replication and failover. Asynchronous replication between regions ensures data consistency, and automated failover mechanisms facilitate seamless transitions in case of disruptions.

Beyond disaster recovery, the cloud enables comprehensive business continuity planning. By architecting applications with fault tolerance in mind, businesses can achieve near-zero downtime and maintain service availability during planned maintenance or unexpected failures.

Regular testing of disaster recovery and business continuity plans is crucial to validate their effectiveness.

Conducting simulated failover exercises allows organizations to identify potential weaknesses and fine-tune their strategies to ensure a swift and effective response to disasters.

In conclusion, cloud governance and risk management are integral to a successful cloud adoption journey. By addressing cloud cost-effectiveness, making informed vendor selections, and ensuring robust disaster recovery and business continuity plans, organizations can navigate the complexities of the cloud era with confidence. Effective cloud governance fosters cost efficiency, agility, and security, enabling businesses to harness the full potential of cloud computing while safeguarding their digital assets and delivering exceptional experiences to users in an ever-changing digital landscape.

CHAPTER V
Cloud-native Technologies and Architecture

A. Microservices and Containerization

In the pursuit of building scalable, agile, and resilient applications, cloud-native technologies have emerged as the cornerstone of modern software development. Among these transformative technologies are microservices and containerization, which revolutionize how applications are designed, deployed, and managed in the cloud era. This chapter explores the fundamentals of microservices architecture, delves into the benefits and challenges of containerization, and introduces Kubernetes as a leading container orchestration solution.

Understanding Microservices Architecture

Microservices architecture is a software development approach that decomposes large, monolithic applications into smaller, loosely coupled services. Each microservice represents a specific business capability and operates independently, communicating with other services via well-defined APIs. This modular and decentralized design fosters flexibility, maintainability, and scalability, allowing teams to develop, deploy, and update services independently without affecting the entire application.

In contrast to traditional monolithic architectures, where changes to one component may necessitate rebuilding and redeploying the entire application, microservices enable continuous delivery and deployment. Developers can focus on specific features or functionalities, accelerating development cycles and facilitating agile methodologies.

The key principles of microservices include:

- Decentralization: Each microservice operates autonomously and has its database, enabling independent scaling and updates.

- Single Responsibility: Microservices are designed to serve a single business capability, ensuring clarity of purpose and reducing complexity.

- Polyglot Persistence: Different microservices may use different databases, allowing teams to choose the best-suited data store for each service's requirements.

- Resilience: With isolated services, the failure of one microservice doesn't bring down the entire application, enhancing overall system resilience.

Benefits and Challenges of Containerization

Containerization has emerged as a fundamental technology in cloud-native development, encapsulating applications and their dependencies in isolated units called containers. Containers are lightweight, portable, and consistent, ensuring that applications run reliably across different environments, from development to production.

The benefits of containerization include:

- Portability: Containers package the application, runtime, libraries, and dependencies, making them highly portable across various cloud platforms and on-premises environments.

- Isolation: Containers provide application isolation, preventing conflicts between applications and enhancing security.

- Resource Efficiency: Due to their lightweight nature, containers require minimal resources and have rapid startup times, optimizing resource utilization.

- Consistency: Containers ensure consistent behavior between development, testing, and production environments, reducing the "it works on my machine" problem.

However, containerization also poses challenges:

- Orchestration: As the number of containers grows, managing and orchestrating them becomes complex. This is where container orchestration solutions, like Kubernetes, play a pivotal role.

- Network Communication: Containers communicate via network ports, which require careful management to ensure secure and efficient inter-service communication.

- Persistent Storage: Containers are ephemeral by design, meaning that data stored within a container is lost when it stops. Managing persistent storage for containers requires careful consideration.

Kubernetes and Container Orchestration

Kubernetes, often referred to as K8s, has emerged as the de facto standard for container orchestration. Developed by Google and later open-sourced, Kubernetes automates the deployment, scaling, and management of containerized applications.

At its core, Kubernetes orchestrates containers across a cluster of nodes, ensuring that applications run smoothly and efficiently. Kubernetes provides several key features that make it an indispensable tool in cloud-native development:

- Deployment: Kubernetes allows declarative updates to applications, enabling easy scaling, rollback, and versioning.

- Scaling: With Kubernetes, applications can scale automatically based on demand, ensuring optimal resource utilization.

- Self-Healing: Kubernetes continuously monitors the health of applications and automatically restarts or replaces failed containers.

- Service Discovery and Load Balancing: Kubernetes automatically assigns IP addresses to containers and load balances network traffic across them.

- Persistent Storage: Kubernetes provides mechanisms for managing and attaching persistent storage to containers, addressing the challenge of data persistence in containerized environments.

Kubernetes' flexibility and extensibility through APIs and custom resources enable developers to build sophisticated, cloud-native architectures. It supports various deployment patterns, including canary releases, blue-green deployments, and more, enabling organizations to roll out new features and updates with minimal disruption.

In conclusion, microservices and containerization represent revolutionary shifts in software development, empowering organizations to build scalable and resilient applications that embrace the cloud-native philosophy. By decomposing monolithic architectures into modular and manageable microservices and harnessing the power of containers, businesses can achieve agility, portability, and efficiency in the cloud era. Kubernetes, as a leading container orchestration platform, provides the essential tools for managing the complexity of containerized environments and enables organizations to fully leverage the transformative potential of cloud-native technologies. As cloud-native principles continue to shape the future of software development, the combination of microservices, containers, and Kubernetes becomes an indispensable blueprint for building the next generation of applications in the interconnected digital landscape.

B. Serverless Computing and Event-Driven Architecture

Cloud-native technologies continue to evolve, introducing new paradigms that reshape application development and deployment. Among these transformative technologies are serverless computing and event-driven architecture, revolutionizing how applications are architected and executed in the cloud era. This chapter explores the concepts of serverless computing, delves into implementing event-driven workflows, and weighs the pros and cons of adopting serverless architectures.

Serverless Computing Concepts

Serverless computing, despite its name, does not mean the absence of servers; rather, it abstracts server management away from developers, allowing them to focus solely on writing application code. In a traditional server-based model, developers need to manage server provisioning, scaling, and maintenance, which can be time-consuming and resource-intensive.

Serverless computing introduces a new execution model where developers write functions that run in response to events, often referred to as "serverless functions" or "function as a service" (FaaS). These functions are stateless and ephemeral, meaning they start, execute a specific task, and shut down once the task is completed. This granular execution eliminates the need to manage servers continuously, as the cloud provider automatically handles the underlying infrastructure.

A key characteristic of serverless is its event-driven nature. Events, such as HTTP requests, database changes, or messages from message queues, trigger the execution of serverless functions. This event-driven approach makes serverless architectures well-suited for handling unpredictable workloads, as resources scale automatically based on incoming events.

Serverless functions are designed to be lightweight and short-lived, making them ideal for executing discrete tasks. Developers can compose these functions into larger workflows to build complex applications without managing the infrastructure complexities.

Implementing Event-Driven Workflows

Event-driven architecture, closely intertwined with serverless computing, enables the design of scalable and loosely coupled systems. In an event-driven architecture, applications communicate and interact through events, allowing components to react to events in real-time.

To implement event-driven workflows, developers define event sources and event handlers. Event sources emit events when specific actions occur, and event handlers are serverless functions that respond to these events. For instance, a user uploading a file to a cloud storage bucket can trigger an event, and a serverless function may process the file and store the result in a database.

Cloud providers offer event-driven services that act as event sources and triggers for serverless functions. These services include AWS Lambda, Azure Functions, Google Cloud Functions, and more, each supporting various event sources, such as API Gateway, Cloud Storage, and database changes.

Event-driven architectures enable applications to be highly responsive and scalable. As events trigger specific actions, components of the application can scale independently based on demand. This loose coupling enhances resilience, as failures in one component do not cascade to others.

Pros and Cons of Serverless Adoption

Serverless computing offers several advantages, making it an attractive option for certain use cases:

- Cost-Efficiency: Serverless functions bill based on execution time, resulting in cost savings for applications with sporadic or low-resource utilization.

- Automatic Scaling: Cloud providers handle scaling of serverless functions, ensuring applications can handle sudden spikes in traffic without manual intervention.

- Focus on Code: Developers can concentrate on writing application logic without worrying about server management, enabling rapid development and deployment.

- Stateless Architecture: Stateless functions simplify development and make applications easier to test and maintain.

However, serverless adoption also presents challenges and considerations:

- Cold Starts: The first invocation of a serverless function after a period of inactivity may experience a "cold start" delay, resulting in slightly higher latency for the first user.

- Execution Limits: Cloud providers impose execution limits on serverless functions, which can affect the processing of long-running tasks.

- Vendor Lock-In: Serverless functions are tied to the specific cloud provider's platform, making it challenging to switch providers once applications are deeply integrated.

- Resource Management: Monitoring and optimizing resource consumption of serverless functions may require specialized tools and approaches.

Choosing a serverless architecture depends on the nature of the application, workload patterns, and performance requirements. Use cases such as event processing, data transformations, and scheduled tasks are well-suited for serverless adoption. Applications with continuous, compute-intensive workloads may benefit from alternative approaches.

In conclusion, serverless computing and event-driven architectures represent transformative paradigms that simplify application development and enable highly responsive and scalable systems. Embracing serverless computing empowers developers to focus on writing code and delivering business value without worrying about server management. Event-driven architectures enhance the responsiveness and resilience of applications by leveraging real-time events to trigger specific actions. While serverless adoption offers significant benefits in terms of cost, scalability, and agility, it also introduces considerations such as cold starts and vendor lock-in. By carefully assessing the suitability of serverless for specific use cases and understanding the implications of this architecture, businesses can leverage the full potential of cloud-native technologies in crafting innovative and efficient applications for the interconnected digital landscape.

CHAPTER VI
The Future of Cloud Computing

A. Trends Shaping the Cloud Landscape

As the digital landscape continues to evolve, the future of cloud computing promises to be dynamic and transformative, driven by emerging technologies and shifting demands. This chapter explores the trends that are shaping the cloud landscape, including edge computing and distributed cloud, the potential impact of quantum computing, and the rise of green cloud initiatives for sustainability.

Edge Computing and Distributed Cloud

Edge computing is a paradigm that brings computation and data storage closer to the location where it is needed, reducing latency and improving real-time processing capabilities. Traditional cloud computing relies on centralized data centers located in specific regions, which may lead to data transmission delays, especially for applications requiring ultra-low latency or handling massive data streams.

The rise of Internet of Things (IoT) devices and real-time applications, such as augmented reality and autonomous vehicles, has driven the need for edge computing. By deploying edge nodes closer to end-users or IoT devices, data can be processed and acted upon locally, enhancing user experience and enabling faster decision-making.

Edge computing complements the cloud by creating a distributed cloud architecture. In this model, cloud services are extended beyond centralized data centers to edge locations, creating a network of interconnected cloud nodes. This distributed cloud approach optimizes data flow and processing, ensuring that data is efficiently processed at the edge while leveraging the cloud's vast computational capabilities for complex workloads.

Quantum Computing and Its Potential Impact

Quantum computing represents a revolutionary advancement in computation, leveraging the principles of quantum mechanics to perform calculations that are currently infeasible for classical computers. Quantum computers have the potential to solve complex problems exponentially faster, which can significantly impact various industries and fields.

In the realm of cloud computing, quantum computing could unleash new possibilities. Quantum computing may enhance encryption and security mechanisms, as it has the potential to break classical encryption algorithms. Conversely, quantum encryption methods can offer unbreakable security for data transmission between cloud nodes.

Quantum computing can also accelerate complex simulations, optimization tasks, and data analytics, transforming industries such as drug discovery, financial modeling, and supply chain optimization. Cloud providers are investing in quantum computing research and development, making quantum computing resources accessible to developers through the cloud.

Green Cloud Initiatives for Sustainability

The increasing demand for cloud services has raised concerns about the environmental impact of data centers, which consume significant amounts of energy.

As cloud computing continues to grow, the industry is taking proactive measures to promote sustainability through green cloud initiatives.

Green cloud initiatives focus on reducing energy consumption, carbon emissions, and electronic waste. Cloud providers are investing in renewable energy sources, such as solar and wind power, to power their data centers. Additionally, providers are exploring innovative cooling techniques and data center designs to improve energy efficiency.

Data center consolidation and server virtualization efforts further contribute to energy savings. By optimizing hardware utilization and decommissioning underutilized servers, cloud providers can reduce the overall carbon footprint of their infrastructure.

Multi-tenancy, where multiple users share the same physical infrastructure, is another practice that promotes resource efficiency and sustainability. Multi-tenancy ensures better utilization of resources, leading to a reduced number of physical servers required to serve multiple customers.

Furthermore, cloud providers are committed to recycling and proper disposal of electronic waste, ensuring that decommissioned hardware is handled responsibly to minimize its environmental impact.

In conclusion, the future of cloud computing is characterized by transformative trends that leverage emerging technologies to shape a more efficient, sustainable, and powerful cloud landscape. Edge computing and distributed cloud bring computation closer to the users, enabling real-time processing and enhancing user experiences. Quantum computing holds the promise of revolutionizing computation capabilities, opening doors to new applications and advancements. Green cloud initiatives highlight the industry's commitment to sustainability, reducing energy consumption, and minimizing the environmental impact of data centers. As cloud computing evolves, businesses, developers, and cloud providers alike stand at the forefront of innovation, embarking on a journey that will redefine the possibilities and potential of the interconnected digital world.

B. Ethical Considerations and the Cloud

As cloud computing continues to shape the future of technology, it brings with it a set of ethical considerations that demand careful attention. This chapter explores the ethical dimensions of the cloud, including AI ethics and responsible data usage, the challenges of the digital divide and inclusivity, and the delicate balance between convenience and privacy in the cloud era.

AI Ethics and Responsible Data Usage

Artificial Intelligence (AI) has become an integral part of cloud computing, powering intelligent applications and services. However, the ethical implications of AI raise important questions about data privacy, bias, and transparency.

AI algorithms often rely on vast amounts of data for training, and this data may include personal and sensitive information. Ethical concerns arise when this data is collected and used without proper consent or when data is used in ways that may harm individuals or perpetuate discrimination.

Responsible data usage involves implementing robust data privacy and protection measures, ensuring data is collected and used only for legitimate purposes with informed consent from users. Cloud providers and developers must prioritize data security, anonymization, and encryption to safeguard user privacy and prevent data breaches.

AI algorithms must also be developed and trained with transparency and fairness in mind. Bias in AI models can lead to discriminatory outcomes, reinforcing social prejudices and inequalities. Ongoing monitoring and auditing of AI systems are necessary to identify and rectify biases, ensuring that AI-driven decisions are equitable and unbiased.

Digital Divide and Inclusivity Challenges

While cloud computing has the potential to empower individuals and organizations worldwide, it also highlights the digital divide and inclusivity challenges. The digital divide refers to the gap between those who have access to technology, including the cloud, and those who do not.

In many regions, limited internet infrastructure and connectivity issues restrict access to the cloud and digital services. This disparity hinders individuals and communities from benefiting from cloud-based resources, creating unequal opportunities in education, employment, and economic development.

Addressing the digital divide requires collaborative efforts from governments, organizations, and technology providers. Initiatives that focus on expanding internet infrastructure, providing affordable connectivity options, and fostering digital literacy are essential to bridge the gap and ensure inclusivity.

Furthermore, inclusivity challenges go beyond access and extend to designing cloud services and applications with diverse user needs in mind. Accessibility features and user-friendly interfaces that cater to individuals with disabilities can enhance the inclusivity of cloud-based solutions, ensuring that everyone can participate in the digital age.

Balancing Convenience with Privacy in the Cloud Era

The cloud era has introduced unparalleled convenience, offering seamless access to applications and services from any device with an internet connection. However, this convenience comes with the trade-off of privacy concerns, as users' data and activities are increasingly stored and processed in cloud environments.

Data privacy is a significant ethical consideration in the cloud era, and it is crucial to strike a balance between convenience and privacy. Cloud providers and developers must adopt a privacy-first mindset, implementing robust privacy controls and giving users the ability to control their data.

Consent management becomes essential in the cloud environment. Users should be clearly informed about data collection practices and have the option to provide informed consent for data processing. Cloud services should offer easy-to-understand privacy settings and granular controls to enable users to manage their data preferences effectively.

Data anonymization and encryption play critical roles in protecting user privacy. Anonymization techniques can be employed to aggregate and process data in a way that prevents individual identification. Encryption ensures that data remains secure and unreadable to unauthorized parties, even if data breaches occur.

As technology advances, it is essential to remain vigilant about potential privacy risks. Artificial Intelligence and Machine Learning, while powerful, can also pose challenges to privacy if used improperly. Striking the right balance between utilizing data for personalized experiences and protecting user privacy is essential for maintaining trust in the cloud ecosystem.

In conclusion, the future of cloud computing comes with a responsibility to address ethical considerations that arise from its widespread adoption. AI ethics and responsible data usage demand transparency, fairness, and protection of user privacy. The digital divide and inclusivity challenges highlight the importance of expanding access and creating inclusive cloud services. Balancing convenience with privacy requires proactive measures to prioritize user data protection and provide users with meaningful control over their information. As cloud computing evolves, embracing ethical principles ensures that technology continues to be a force for positive change, enabling a future where the cloud is not only innovative and transformative but also ethical and inclusive for all.

CHAPTER VII
Case Studies of Cloud Success Stories

A. Cloud Adoption in Large Enterprises

Cloud computing has revolutionized the way large enterprises approach technology, offering scalability, flexibility, and cost-effectiveness. This chapter showcases success stories of cloud adoption by three tech giants: Amazon Web Services (AWS), Microsoft Azure, and Google Cloud Platform (GCP). These case studies highlight how these cloud providers have helped enterprises transform their operations, innovate, and achieve unprecedented levels of growth and efficiency.

Amazon Web Services (AWS) Case Study

AWS, a subsidiary of Amazon, is a leading cloud computing platform that has played a pivotal role in enabling businesses to harness the full potential of the cloud. One notable success story is that of Netflix, the world's largest subscription-based streaming service.

Before migrating to AWS, Netflix faced challenges in delivering content efficiently and scaling its infrastructure to meet growing demand. The company needed a robust, scalable, and cost-effective solution to serve its global audience. AWS provided the ideal platform for Netflix's needs.

By leveraging AWS's vast network of data centers and content delivery services, Netflix improved the streaming experience for its users worldwide. AWS's ability to handle peak loads during high-demand events, such as premieres and major content releases, ensured seamless streaming without interruptions.

Additionally, AWS enabled Netflix to optimize costs through on-demand scaling. The company could provision resources as needed, avoiding overprovisioning and unnecessary expenses. This flexibility allowed Netflix to allocate its resources more effectively, focusing on innovation and content creation.

AWS's comprehensive security features and compliance certifications also provided Netflix with the confidence that user data and intellectual property were well-protected. This was crucial in maintaining the trust of millions of subscribers.

Microsoft Azure Success Stories

Microsoft Azure has been at the forefront of cloud innovation, empowering businesses to accelerate their digital transformation journeys. One remarkable success story comes from GE Healthcare, a leading provider of medical imaging and digital solutions.

GE Healthcare sought to develop and deploy cloud-based applications that would enhance patient care and drive medical advancements. The company needed a cloud platform that could support complex medical imaging workloads and ensure data security and compliance.

Azure's powerful cloud infrastructure and compliance certifications made it an ideal choice for GE Healthcare. With Azure's extensive global presence, GE Healthcare could deploy applications closer to healthcare providers and patients, reducing latency and improving data accessibility.

Azure's AI and machine learning capabilities also played a significant role in GE Healthcare's success. By leveraging Azure's advanced analytics tools, GE Healthcare could process and analyze medical data more efficiently, leading to faster diagnoses and more personalized treatments.

Moreover, Azure's commitment to data privacy and security aligned with GE Healthcare's stringent compliance requirements in the healthcare industry. This ensured that sensitive patient data remained protected and adhered to the industry's strict regulatory standards.

Google Cloud Platform (GCP) Case Study

Google Cloud Platform (GCP) has emerged as a prominent cloud provider, offering cutting-edge technologies and innovation to businesses worldwide. One remarkable success story is that of Spotify, the popular music streaming service.

Before adopting GCP, Spotify faced challenges in managing and scaling its vast infrastructure to accommodate millions of users and deliver music seamlessly. GCP provided Spotify with the tools and capabilities necessary to overcome these challenges.

GCP's data analytics and machine learning offerings played a vital role in enhancing Spotify's user experience. By leveraging GCP's data processing capabilities, Spotify gained insights into user preferences and behavior, enabling personalized music recommendations and playlists.

GCP's scalable infrastructure allowed Spotify to accommodate surges in user traffic during major music events, such as album releases or exclusive artist performances. The ability to scale quickly and cost-effectively ensured a smooth streaming experience for Spotify's global user base.

Moreover, GCP's data storage and management services helped Spotify handle vast amounts of music data efficiently. This enabled faster content delivery and reduced the time taken to load songs, leading to improved user satisfaction.

Additionally, GCP's commitment to sustainability aligned with Spotify's environmental goals. GCP's data centers are designed for energy efficiency, contributing to Spotify's efforts to reduce its carbon footprint.

In conclusion, the case studies of AWS, Microsoft Azure, and Google Cloud Platform demonstrate the transformative power of cloud computing for large enterprises. These cloud providers have empowered businesses to achieve unprecedented levels of scalability, cost-efficiency, and innovation. The success stories of Netflix, GE Healthcare, and Spotify showcase the potential of cloud adoption to revolutionize industries and enhance user experiences. As the cloud landscape continues to evolve, large enterprises can continue to leverage these cloud platforms to drive their digital transformation journeys and remain at the forefront of innovation in the interconnected world.

B. Cloud Empowering Startups and Small Businesses

Cloud computing has democratized technology, allowing startups and small businesses to access enterprise-grade capabilities without significant upfront investments. This chapter showcases success stories of how cloud adoption has empowered startups and small businesses, enabling scalability, driving innovation, and implementing cost-saving strategies.

Scalability Benefits for Growing Companies

One prime example of how cloud computing empowers startups and small businesses is the success story of Airbnb, the global online vacation rental marketplace. As Airbnb experienced exponential growth, it needed a robust infrastructure to handle increasing user demands and accommodate a rapidly expanding host and guest base.

By leveraging the scalability of cloud services, Airbnb was able to dynamically provision computing resources based on demand. During peak booking seasons and major events, the platform could seamlessly scale its infrastructure to handle a surge in traffic without worrying about capacity planning.

Moreover, as Airbnb expanded globally, cloud providers' distributed data centers allowed the platform to serve users in multiple regions efficiently. This global reach enabled Airbnb to deliver content and provide localized experiences tailored to each market.

The scalability of cloud services also enabled Airbnb to experiment with new features and quickly iterate on its platform. This agility played a crucial role in refining user experiences, driving engagement, and staying ahead of the competition.

Cloud-Based Innovations and Disruptive Startups

Cloud computing has been a catalyst for disruptive startups, fueling innovation and challenging traditional business models. One compelling example is Slack, the cloud-based collaboration and communication platform that transformed how teams work together.

Before Slack, traditional enterprise communication tools were often cumbersome and lacked integration with other applications. Slack's cloud-based approach addressed these pain points, offering real-time messaging, file sharing, and integrations with popular productivity tools.

By adopting cloud technology, Slack delivered a seamless user experience across various devices and platforms. Teams could collaborate in real-time, share information effortlessly, and reduce reliance on email, fostering productivity and efficiency.

Slack's disruptive model also extended to its business strategy. The freemium approach allowed startups and small businesses to experience the benefits of Slack before committing to paid plans. This user-centric approach contributed to rapid adoption and growth.

Cost-Saving Strategies with Cloud Services

For startups and small businesses with limited budgets, cost optimization is crucial for sustainable growth. Cloud services offer cost-saving strategies that can be game-changers for these businesses.

A noteworthy case study is that of Dropbox, the cloud storage and file-sharing service. Dropbox's early adoption of cloud technology allowed it to scale cost-effectively and offer competitive pricing to its users.

Cloud storage eliminates the need for on-premises storage infrastructure, reducing hardware and maintenance costs for startups. Dropbox leveraged cloud storage to store users' files securely, providing them with convenient access across devices without the burden of maintaining physical servers.

Additionally, cloud providers offer a pay-as-you-go pricing model, where businesses pay only for the resources they consume. This eliminates the need for upfront capital expenditures, making cloud services accessible to startups and small businesses with limited resources.

Furthermore, cloud services enable businesses to scale their resources up or down based on demand, ensuring cost efficiency during both high and low activity periods. This flexibility allows startups to manage costs effectively, avoiding unnecessary expenses during idle periods.

In conclusion, cloud computing has democratized technology, empowering startups and small businesses with enterprise-grade capabilities. The success stories of Airbnb, Slack, and Dropbox exemplify how cloud adoption drives scalability, innovation, and cost optimization for growing companies. Scalability benefits enable startups to handle rapid growth and serve a global user base seamlessly. Cloud-based innovations empower disruptive startups to challenge traditional business models and revolutionize industries. Cost-saving strategies provided by cloud services allow startups and small businesses to operate efficiently within budget constraints. As cloud technology continues to evolve, it will undoubtedly play a pivotal role in shaping the future of startups and small businesses, enabling them to thrive and make a lasting impact in the dynamic and interconnected digital landscape.

Conclusion

A. Recapitulation of the Cloud Revolution's Impact

The cloud revolution has left an indelible mark on the technology landscape, fundamentally transforming the way businesses and individuals interact with data, applications, and services. This revolution has ushered in an era of unprecedented connectivity, scalability, and innovation, revolutionizing industries across the globe.

The introduction of cloud computing has been a game-changer for large enterprises, startups, and small businesses alike. Large enterprises have embraced cloud adoption to leverage its scalability, flexibility, and cost-effectiveness, enabling them to meet growing demands and expand their global reach. Case studies of industry giants such as Netflix, GE Healthcare, and Spotify demonstrate how cloud platforms like Amazon Web Services (AWS), Microsoft Azure, and Google Cloud Platform (GCP) have revolutionized their operations and empowered them to deliver exceptional services to millions of users worldwide.

For startups and small businesses, the cloud has leveled the playing field, providing access to enterprise-grade technologies without the burden of extensive upfront investments. Companies like Airbnb, Slack, and Dropbox exemplify how cloud computing has enabled disruptive innovations, driving growth and challenging traditional business models. Scalability benefits have allowed these startups to handle rapid expansion and accommodate a global user base seamlessly.

The cloud revolution has not only transformed how businesses operate but has also reshaped the digital ecosystem. Digital transformation initiatives have been accelerated by cloud adoption, enabling organizations to embrace emerging technologies such as Artificial Intelligence, Internet of Things, and Big Data analytics. Cloud-native technologies like microservices, containerization, and serverless computing have become essential for building agile and resilient applications that power the digital age.

Throughout this journey, ethical considerations have emerged as critical factors that must be addressed in the cloud era. AI ethics, data privacy, inclusivity, and environmental sustainability have become important focal points for cloud providers, developers, and users to ensure technology is used responsibly and inclusively.

Looking to the future, the cloud landscape promises to be even more dynamic and transformative. Edge computing and distributed cloud will continue to evolve, bringing computation closer to users and enabling real-time processing for IoT and immersive experiences. Quantum computing has the potential to revolutionize computation and drive breakthroughs in various industries. Cloud providers' commitment to sustainability will lead to greener data centers and environmentally responsible practices.

In conclusion, the cloud revolution has redefined the boundaries of what is possible in the digital age. From large enterprises to startups, cloud adoption has unlocked a new realm of possibilities, fostering innovation, efficiency, and inclusivity. As the cloud landscape continues to evolve, the potential for transformative impact remains boundless. Embracing the cloud revolution's opportunities responsibly, ethically, and sustainably will shape a future where technology continues to be a driving force for positive change, empowering individuals and organizations in the interconnected and ever-evolving digital world.

B. Looking Ahead: Cloud's Role in the Digital Future

As we conclude our exploration of the cloud revolution and its impact, it is evident that the cloud's role in shaping the digital future is set to be transformative and far-reaching. Cloud computing has become an indispensable pillar of the modern technological landscape, and its influence will only continue to grow in the years to come.

The digital future will be characterized by even greater reliance on cloud computing as organizations, governments, and individuals seek to harness its power for innovation and efficiency. Cloud-native technologies, such as microservices, containerization, and serverless computing, will become the foundation of software development, enabling agile and scalable applications that adapt to ever-changing demands.

Edge computing and distributed cloud will further revolutionize how we interact with technology, bringing computation and data closer to end-users and devices. The proliferation of Internet of Things (IoT) devices, autonomous vehicles, and smart cities will rely heavily on edge computing to deliver real-time insights and experiences.

Quantum computing, still in its early stages, holds immense promise for solving complex problems that were once thought to be insurmountable. Cloud providers' continued investment in quantum computing research and accessibility will open up new possibilities across industries, from drug discovery to supply chain optimization.

Ethical considerations will remain at the forefront of cloud technology's development. Ensuring AI ethics, data privacy, inclusivity, and sustainability will be critical in building a responsible digital future. Cloud providers will play a vital role in fostering trust through transparent practices and robust security measures.

The cloud's role in the digital future extends beyond businesses and enterprises. Educational institutions, healthcare providers, and government agencies will increasingly leverage cloud computing to modernize their services, drive efficiencies, and deliver better outcomes for citizens and users.

In this digital future, cloud computing will democratize access to technology, bridging the digital divide and fostering inclusivity. Small businesses and startups will continue to flourish, enabled by cloud services that empower them with the capabilities previously available only to large enterprises.

Ultimately, the cloud revolution is not just about technology; it is about the potential for positive impact on individuals' lives and society as a whole. Embracing cloud technologies responsibly and ethically will pave the way for a digital future that is more interconnected, intelligent, and sustainable.

As we look ahead, it is clear that the cloud's journey has only just begun. The transformative power of cloud computing will continue to shape the way we live, work, and connect in the digital age. As technology evolves and new challenges arise, the cloud will remain an ever-present force, empowering us to explore uncharted territories and realize the boundless possibilities of the interconnected world.

C. Embracing the Potential and Navigating Challenges

The cloud revolution has undeniably unleashed a wave of potential that has transformed the technological landscape. It offers unprecedented opportunities for businesses, governments, and individuals to innovate, scale, and connect like never before. However, with this potential also come challenges that must be navigated to ensure a responsible and inclusive digital future.

Embracing the potential of the cloud involves recognizing its transformative capabilities and harnessing them to drive positive change. For businesses, cloud adoption is no longer an option but a necessity to remain competitive and agile in a rapidly evolving marketplace. Embracing cloud-native technologies empowers developers to build efficient, scalable, and resilient applications that can adapt to dynamic demands.

Governments and institutions can leverage cloud computing to modernize their operations, provide citizen-centric services, and foster digital inclusivity. Cloud-based innovations can transform education, healthcare, and public services, enhancing accessibility and efficiency.

The cloud also holds promise for addressing global challenges such as climate change and sustainable development. Cloud providers' commitment to environmental sustainability through green initiatives and renewable energy usage aligns with efforts to reduce the carbon footprint of technology.

However, navigating the challenges associated with the cloud era is equally crucial. Data privacy and security must remain paramount, as the cloud holds vast amounts of personal and sensitive information. Cloud providers and users must prioritize strong security measures, encryption, and compliance with data protection regulations to safeguard user trust.

Ethical considerations must be at the forefront of AI and machine learning implementations. Ensuring fairness, transparency, and accountability in AI algorithms is essential to prevent biases and discriminatory outcomes.

Additionally, the digital divide remains a critical challenge that demands attention. Bridging the gap between those who have access to the cloud and technology and those who do not is crucial for creating an inclusive digital society. Efforts to expand internet infrastructure, increase digital literacy, and provide affordable connectivity options are essential for ensuring that no one is left behind in the digital age.

Vendor lock-in and interoperability concerns also require careful consideration. While cloud platforms offer an array of services, businesses and organizations must assess their cloud strategies to avoid dependencies that may hinder flexibility and portability.

As the cloud landscape continues to evolve, collaboration between cloud providers, businesses, and regulators is vital to address emerging challenges and shape responsible practices. Cloud users must stay informed about updates and advancements in cloud technology to make informed decisions that align with their needs and values.

In conclusion, embracing the potential of the cloud revolution while navigating challenges is essential for creating a digital future that benefits society as a whole. Cloud computing empowers us to imagine and implement innovative solutions to complex problems, but it also demands responsible and ethical practices to ensure trust and inclusivity. By embracing the potential of the cloud and collaborating to address challenges, we can collectively shape a future where technology serves as a driving force for positive change, fostering a connected, sustainable, and equitable digital world.